Marijuana
BUDS
for less

Grow 8 oz. of bud for less than $100

by SeeMoreBuds

Marijuana Buds for Less

Grow 8 oz. of bud for less than $100

Copyright © 2007 SeeMoreBuds

Published by Quick American

A division of Quick Trading Co.

Oakland, California

ISBN 978-0-932551-87-0

ISBN 10: 0-932551-87-4

Executive Editor: Ed Rosenthal

Cover and Interior Design: Hera Lee

All photos: SeeMoreBuds

Printed in China

This is a personal grow journal showing the absolute easiest way to grow an amazing plant. All the details have been recorded so that it can be replicated. Just turn the pages, one day at a time. Peace & Love, SeeMoreBuds

These are the six ingredients for a simple, successful grow.

    1. 42 watt Compact Fluorescent Bulbs (CFL)—at least 6, with light fixtures and reflective hoods (the reflectors are not shown in following photos so that the position of the lights can be clearly seen).

    2. A container with drainage holes—1-5 gallon pots (4-20 L) are suitable; 3 gallon (10 L) containers are ideal.

    3. Potting soil (medium which your plant will grow in). If soil does not contain fertilizer you will need to add a time release fertilizer.

    4. A timer to control the light cycle (with at least one On and one Off setting per 24 hours).

    5. Rockwool cube to start your seed in—helpful, but not necessary for seed propagation (optional).

    6. Perlite—used for drainage at the bottom of the container and helps aeration in soil (optional).

Additional supplies: fans, odor eating lights, pest strips, CO_2 bucket, thermometer.

Preparing a pot is a simple procedure but can mean the difference between success and failure. The pot and the soil are the plant's food and shelter. A thriving plant must have a good home with access to adequate food. The Miracle Grow soil used here comes with a time release fertilizer. If your soil does not, mix in a time release fertilizer.

1. Use a simple plastic pot with a drainage hole; a 3 gallon (10 L) container is ideal. 2. Put a piece of newspaper at the bottom to prevent the growing medium from spilling out, but still allowing water to drain. 3. Fill bottom of the pot with ½ inch (1 cm) of perlite—this helps with drainage and root aeration. 4. Mix 80% soil, 20% perlite and fill your pot with it. Leave ½ to 1 inch (1-2.5 cm) of space at the top of the pot. 5. Put your seed ¼ inch (6 mm) into the rockwool cube. You may also place the seed directly into the soil. 6. Water the cube and soil using ½-gallon (1.2 liters) or more of 7.4 pH balanced water—if you are using Miracle Grow. If not, check the pH of your soil and adjust accordingly (see chart on pg. v). Your soil and cube should be thoroughly saturated and water drain from the bottom of the container. Keep the seed moist with daily watering of 1/16 cup (14 mL) of water until the seed germinates (less water may be required to keep the rockwool cube moist).

Watering technique is very important. This is a root ball of a plant that was watered correctly (3). (The colored area is the newspaper used to cover the drainage hole.) Notice how the roots have utilized all the soil. When plants are not watered properly, roots will accumulate on the bottom of the container. This will eventually cause the plant to become root bound and require the plant to be transplanted. Transplanting can be avoided if one waters thoroughly and only when required. You can see a plant that clearly needs water by looking at its leaves (1). Droopy, soft leaves are a sign of a thirsty plant. You can see the change in the plant just 30 minutes after it was watered (2). A plant can also have soft and droopy leaves if it is over watered. Checking your soil regularly will help you decide if your plant needs water. Stick your finger into the soil and if the top 2-4 inches (5-10 cm) are dry, the plant most likely needs watering. (You may also use a moisture meter.) A cannabis plant kept at 70-80° F (21-27° C) will need watering every 3-10 days depending on its size and the stage of its life cycle. With experience and increased plant awareness, you will develop and cultivate a relationship and understanding of your plant's needs.

A pH tester is a grower's best friend. They range in price from \$3 to \$300. pH level is the measurement of acidity and affects a plant's ability to absorb nutrients (eat food). The ideal pH level for a cannabis plant in soil is between 5.9 and 6.5 (for hydro grows, optimum pH is between 5.9 to 6.3). Water is the vehicle in which plants receive their food. Therefore the pH of the water must be set between 6.0 and 6.5. Making perfectly pH balanced water is easy and essential for a successful grow.

Fill a bucket with water, get a sample of the water and add pH test solution (1). Compare the color of the treated water to the chart on the back of the tester (2, 3). A vial pH tester is suitable for beginners and professionals; however, electronic meters are not necessarily costly and are very accurate (4). If the pH needs to be lowered, add a small amount of vinegar or pH Down. If the pH needs to be raised, add baking soda or pH Up (5, 6). Retest and repeat this process until you get the desired pH.

NOTE: *Because the Miracle Grow soil used in this book has a pH of 5.1, the water used to grow this plant was adjusted accordingly. Watering done in the first half of the plants life was adjusted to a pH of 7.4.*

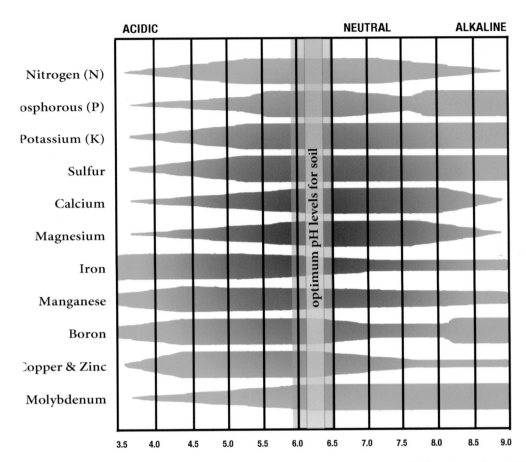

Plant nutrient availability: the chart above shows which nutrients your plant will absorb at what pH level. Optimum pH levels for cannabis soil grows are between 5.9 and 6.0 (blue band); 6.2 or 6.3 is ideal.

Soil	5.1	5.2	5.3	5.4	5.5	5.6	5.7	5.8.	5.9	6.0	6.1
Water	7.4	7.3	7.2	7.1	7.0	6.9	6.8	6.7	6.6	6.5	6.4

Achieving the perfect pH: the pH of the soil determines the best pH of the water. If the pH of the soil is unknown, adjust the water's pH to 6.5. pH levels are the foundation of your empire; a perfect pH is a perfect foundation.

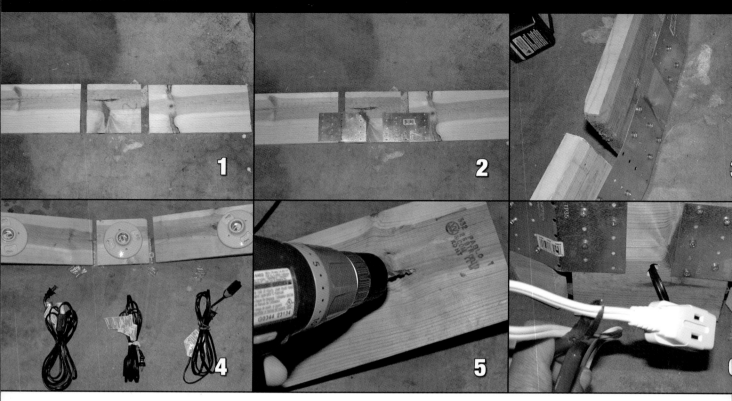

This is a basic light set up. The goal is to build a fixture that is inexpensive, easy to adjust, provides adequate light and can be easily modified for additional lights.

(1), (2) and (3): Three pieces of wood are screwed together using two flexible pieces of metal. These pre-drilled pieces of sheet metal can be purchased at any hardware store. They are flexible enough to bend for easy light adjustment yet strong enough to hold a rigid shape. A ½-inch space (1 cm) is left between the pieces of wood to allow for easy bending. (4). Three extension cords and three fixtures will be attached to the wooden frame. (5). Drill a hole in each board directly behind the location where you will be mounting the light fixture to the wood. (6). Cut the female end off the extension cord to expose 2 wires.

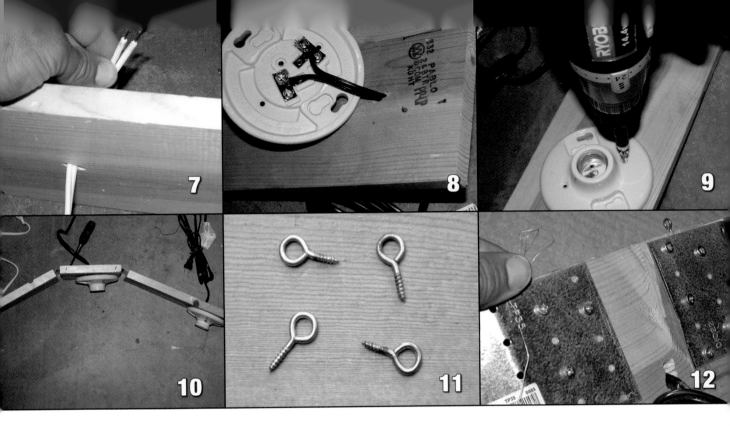

(7). Pull wire through hole and strip the ends. (8). Attach wires to the light fixture. (9). Secure light fixture to the board. (10). The fixture is nearly complete. (11). Eyelets are attached on all 4 corners of the center piece of wood. (12). Fasten wire or string to the eyelets so that you can hang the fixture.

The finished fixture is functional and easy to maneuver. There are four different attachment points from which the fixture hangs. The multiple points provide stability and ensures that the light will not fall on the precious and valuable plant below. The lighting at different heights and angles will provide better light coverage to the plant and thus increase the yield. More light gets to the plant if simple light reflectors are used; reflectors are not shown in these photographs to better show the position of the lighting assembly.

Alternating Nodes: *When leaves grow at different heights on the axis, not directly opposite each other but in succession, alternating sides.*

Blue Dot: *This is a California Medical Strain found at many of dispensaries. A med patient in Sonoma created it. It was originally called MGB, for Medical Grade Bud; primarily Sativa.*

Clone: *A genetically identical copy.*

Cloning: *Taking cuttings from a mother plant and making clones.*

Flowering Stage: *This is the last stage of a plant. It produces seeds and fruit in this stage. Changing of seasons, shorter days and shorter light periods trigger flowering. It is critical that a plant gets at least 12 hours of uninterrupted darkness every 24 hours to induce flowering.*

Indica: *Short thick plants, broad leaves, darker green, flavors from stinky skunk to fruity sweet. Origins traced back to Afghanistan, Nepal and Tibet. More of a body stone. Indoor grower's favorite types.*

Lumen: *The unit of measure for the light energy which flows in air.*

Mango: *Mango is a versatile plant that can be grown indoors as well as outdoors. The buds are very large, like Big Bud, and harvest is early with high yields. Mango's buds are colorful and her taste is sweet. If you like Bubblegum or Juicy Fruit, you will like Mango.*

Mother Plant: *A plant that is kept in a vegetative stage and used for cloning.*

Necrotic: *Discolored, dead.*

Nodes: *The point on a stem where a leaf is attached or has been attached; joint.*

Pistils: *The female organs of a flower.*

Secondary Growth: *The branch growing off of a branch that comes from the main stalk.*

Sensemilla: *Flowering tops which are free of seeds from being grown in a pollen-free environment.*

Stretch: *The growth of spacing between nodes. Usually stretching is exaggerated when there is a shortage of light.*

Vegetative Stage: *This is the primary growth stage of a plant. The plant needs to be under 18-24 or hours of light to stay in this stage.*

Introduction—

This book is a daily journal of plants from seed to harvest. Each journal entry provides you with pictures that allow you to visually compare your plant's progress with those of SeeMoreBuds. You also get all the instruction needed to take care of a plant. These instructons will walk you through the day to day care and attention that your plant needs.

Each page contains historical, scientific or cultural facts about marijuana. Each day also has a simple quote of eternal truth. Being able to hear these quotes uses the same awareness required to know your plant. Knowing your plant is extremely beneficial as questions arise regarding the plant's health and condition.

Marijuana is one of the most commonly used drugs in the world, following only caffeine, nicotine, and alcoholic beverages in popularity.

www.encyclopedia.com

Place a seed or a clone into a rockwool cube or other growing medium. Keep the rockwool moist at all times before germination. This is a Mango seed just hours after it cracked (2,3). The seed was planted 5 days earlier, ¼ inch (6 mm) inside the rockwool cube. A 42 watt compact fluorescent light (CFL) is hung 2-3 inches (5-7 cm) from the baby sprout (1). This light was turned on (18 hours a day) before the seed sprouted in order to keep the rockwool cube warm. Seeds take 24 hours to 2 weeks to germinate (5-7 days is normal). A clone (1) is being grown under a similar set up. In the next 5-7 days, the CFL will be kept 3 inches (8 cm) from the foliage. The closer the light is to the plant, the more light the plant is receiving. More light means more growth. It is very important to keep CFL's as close as possible to (without touching) your mature plants.

To meet everything and everyone through stillness instead of mental noise is the greatest gift you can give the universe.
-Eckhart Tolle

DAY
2

The earliest dates associated with marijuana are "7000-8000 B.C. First woven fabric is believed to be from hemp."

DrugWarRant.com
by Peter Guither

This too shall pass.
-Buddha

The cube is kept moist and the light is kept on 24 hours a day (the CFL is never turned off). The plant pushes towards the sky and reveals its embryonic leaves (cotyledons). If you are growing without a rockwool cube and have planted your seed directly in the soil, you may need to water your plant with a few tablespoons of water every day to keep the young tender roots of your seedling from drying out. Young roots need to be moist. As long as you only use a few tablespoons (milliliters) a day, you will not have to worry about over watering. The CFL should be approximately 2-3 inches (5-7 cm) from the seedling.

In modern times a person in the United States of America is arrested every 42 seconds on marijuana charges, 2004.

www.wikipedia.org

The plant stands 2 inches (5 cm) tall and has completely opened its first set of true leaves, which are single bladed and serrated. Photosynthesis is the process whereby light is converted into chemical energy that the plant can use. Optimal photosynthesis for cannabis occurs at a 74-80° F (23-27° C). Any temperature below 65 or above 80° F (below 18 or above 29° C) is asking for trouble. Hot temperatures are ideal for bugs. Cool temperatures promote mold/fungus and dramatically slow growth. Drastic changes in day/night temperature can cause moisture, which encourages fungus and mold. Keeping the temperature below 80° F (27° C) can be a challenge for growers who are confined to small indoor spaces. Use oscillating fans to keep air moving; fans do not have to be pointed directly at your plant. Fortunately, CFL's emit very little heat.

Do you have the patience to wait till your mud settles and the water is clear? Can you remain unmoving till the right action arises by itself?
-Lao Tzu

3

DAY
4

A third set of leaves arrived today. The temperature in the room was dipping below 70° F (21° C). Rather than put in a heater, more lights were added.

The lights remedied the temperature problem. More light will also increase the total yield and quality of the yield. The seedling was checked every couple hours for the first day to make sure that these additional lights did not add too much heat. Special care and attention should be given to seedlings. Too much heat can kill a seedling in less than an hour. A mature cannabis plant is extremely hardy and can withstand days without proper care.

Unsubstantiated statements made by Director of Federal Bureau of Narcotics Harry J. Anslinger in 1930 - "Reefer makes darkies think they're as good as white men." and "Marijuana is the most violence-causing drug in the history of mankind."

The larger pot on the left (1) is the Mango seedling. The two plants to the right of the Mango are clones that are being grown simultaneously under the same CFL's. There are eight CFL's in this small area. You can grow with as few as one CFL. The fixtures have all been split (2,3) so that they can accommodate two bulbs per fixture. Each 42 watt CFL puts out 2700 lumens.

Nature is trying very hard to make us succeed, but nature does not depend on us. We are not the only experiement.
-Buckminster Fuller

DAY 6

Based upon the facts established in this record and set out above, one must reasonably conclude that there is accepted safety for use of marijuana under medical supervision.

Highlight from the Judge's decision in: Alliance for Cannabis Therapeutics vs. US Drug Enforcement Administration

Advance, and never halt, for advancing is perfection. Advance and do not fear the thorns in the path, for they draw only corrupt blood.
-Kahlil Gibran

Seedlings need water every couple days so that the young fragile roots do not dry out. The soil should be moist but not soggy or muddy. The Mango is watered with ½ cup (120 mL) of 7.4 pH water directly onto the rockwool cube. Normally the pH of the water would be between 6.0 and 6.5. The pH of Miracle Grow Soil is so low, the first few waterings will have a pH set at 7.4. The plant is leaving the seedling stage and is entering the vegetative stage. The Mango is quickly growing an extensive root system.

DAY
7

In 1976, the Dutch government decided to treat possession and cultivation of up to 30 grams as activities "not for prosecution, detection or arrest." This policy of tolerance paved the way for the "coffee shop system" of publicly distributing both marijuana and hashish.

www.drugpolicy.org/marijuana

The two true sets of leaves have grown steadily for the past 3 days. You can see the Blue Dot clones are much larger than the Mango (2). It is too early to tell if the Mango is female or male. The female cannabis plant produces harvestable buds to smoke. Male plants produce pollen and are disposed of by most gardeners. If a female plant gets pollinated by a male plant, the female plant will produce buds with seeds. Marijuana with seeds is considered unacceptable by most growers. Plants will not show their sex until they reach maturity or are forced into the flowering stage.

In three words I can sum up everything I've learned about life: it goes on.
-Robert Frost

DAY
8

The way bhakti works, you just love until you and the beloved become one.
-Ram Dass

The seedling is given a cup (236 ml) of 7.4 pH water. Watering from this point forward will follow the correct watering procedure as explained on page iv.

"Reefer makes darkies think they're as good as white men." and "Marijuana is the most violence-causing drug in the history of mankind."

-unsubstantiated statements made by Director of Federal Bureau of Narcotics Harry J. Anslinger in 1930

Your plant has survived germination! The delicate seedling stage has come to an end. When the plant is approximately 14 days old it will begin to grow at a dramatic pace, an inch (2.5 cm) a day. It will quickly resemble a small bush. This period of a plant's life is called the vegetative stage. During this vigorous growing period it is important that the lights are as close to the foliage as possible—3 inches (7.5 cm). If the lights are not close enough to the foliage, the plant will begin to stretch.

When I met my Guru, he told me: "You are not what you take yourself to be. Find out what you are. Watch the sense 'I am', find your real Self." I obeyed him....All my spare time I would spend looking at myself in silence. And what a difference it made, and how soon!
-Nisargadatta Maharaj

DAY
10

THC in marijuana is rapidly absorbed by fatty tissues in various organs. Generally, traces of THC can be detected by standard urine testing methods several days after a smoking session. However, in chronic heavy users, traces can sometimes be detected for weeks after they have stopped using marijuana.

www.people.howstuffworks.com

Today the seedling was watered thoroughly with 2 quarts (1.9 liters) of water. The pH of the water was set to 6.8. Several cups of water ran out the bottom of the pot and into the catch tray. The run off was left in the catch tray. One hour later all the water in the catch tray was gone. It was absorbed through the drainage holes into the growing medium. The temperature in the closet stays between 69 and 75° F (21-24° C). The water is no longer poured directly onto the rockwool cube. The water is poured evenly around the surface of the soil avoiding direct contact with the rockwool cube. Continuous moisture around the stem of a mature plant can lead to stem rot.

In 1937, Congress passed the Marijuana Tax Act. The statute effectively criminalized marijuana, restricting possession to ndividuals who paid an excise tax for certain authorized medical and industrial uses.

The red arrow (1) is pointing at the plant's first set of nodes. This spot is one of the key indicators of a plant's health. This point on a plant should remain green throughout the plant's entire life span. Except for a few less popular strains, a healthy cannabis plant will always have green stalks and stems. Red stems are generally a sign that the cannabis plant has some sort of nutrient deficiency. Nutrient deficiencies are often caused by pH levels that fall outside the levels that best suit a cannabis plant (5.9-6.5).

People only see what they are prepared to see.
-Ralph Waldo Emerson

DAY
12

The number of laws is constantly growing in all countries and, owing to this, what is called crime is very often not a crime at all, for it contains no element of violence or harm.
-P. D. Ouspensky

The Mango on the left, in the 3 gallon (11.4 liter) pot, could easily be grown in an area as small as 2 x 2 feet (60 x 60 cm). For ease of taking pictures and writing this book a much larger space was used. In the back right hand corner there is a thermometer. Maintaining optimal temperatures of 70-80° F (21-27° C) encourages fast growth and reduces the risk of mold or mildew infections.

Direct health care costs of substance abuse in 2002 in Canada was $39,800,000,000.00: $17 billion—Smoking; 14.6 billion—Alcohol; $8.2 billion—Illegal drugs such as cocaine, heroin, crack, etc. combined; *$0—Marijuana*

www.canada.com [with edits]

The plant's second set of nodes are circled in red. These nodes are opposite each other. When a plant reaches maturity it will grow alternating nodes.

This is the way of peace: Overcome evil with good, and falsehood with truth, and hatred with love."
-Peace Pilgrim

DAY
14

[E]scalating marijuana arrests over the past two decades have failed to have any impact on marijuana use rates or other indicators chosen by drug enforcers to measure "success"...

www.stopthedrugwar.org

A day will dawn when you will laugh at your past efforts. What you realize on the day you laugh is also here and now.
-Ramana Maharshi

The Mango continues to grow new sets of healthy leaves (3,4). The Mango's first set of fan leaves have grown across the diameter of the 3 gallon pot (11.4 liters) (2).

Mariuana might contain compounds that slow memory loss in Alzheimer's patients, according to a new study that bolsters other research suggesting potential brain benefits of pot.

livescience.com

The only way around is through.
-Robert Frost

A healthy plant in its vegetative state grows vigorously. Each new set of fan leaves will be larger and have more serrated blades than the previous set. New growth should always be bigger. This is a key indicator of a healthy plant. If new growth appears weak and smaller than the previous set of fan leaves, it is nearly certain that there is a problem. Most problems occur because of improper pH, over watering or over feeding.

DAY 16

Hemp is cannabis grown specifically for industrial use and thus contains very low levels of cannabinoids (THC). Properly grown hemp has virtually no psychoactive (intoxicating) effects when consumed. Hemp is among the most productive and useful plants known.

www.hempnation.com

The unexamined life is not worth living.
-Socrates, 399 BC

The Mango is 4.5 inches (11.4 cm) tall and has four fully developed sets of leaves. It is still 4-6 weeks from reaching maturity. Growth is extremely fast and the plant's fan leaves have grown out beyond the perimeter of the pot. In nature this plant would continue with its vegetative stage for 4-12 additional weeks. It would grow into a massive plant 4-15 feet (1.2-4.5 meters) tall and the sun would provide more than adequate light for the dense plant. The complete life cycle from germination through flowering can take more than 20 weeks. Today the plant was forced into its flowering stage at only 16 days old. The timer was adjusted so that the lights are on for 12 hours and off for 12 hours. The plant will not produce buds without 12 hours of uninterrupted darkness every 24 hours.

[W]e did not find any evidence for an increase in cancer risk for even heavy marijuana smoking. Cellular studies and even some studies in animal models suggest that THC has anti-tumor properties....

Donald Tashkin, MD (Pulmonary specialist and Federal Government researcher finds marijuana does not cause lung cancer in his study on the effects of cannabis and the lungs.)

Why force the plant out of its vegetative stage and into the flowering stage so early? CFL lights have limited penetration. They cannot maintain a healthy plant larger than 20 inches (51 cm) in height. Many new indoor growers think a bigger plant means more buds. Well, they may be right, but more buds do not mean a larger yield (more weight). A large plant grown under CFL's may have many small fluffy buds, most weighing less than .5 grams (.018 ounces). A smaller plant can produce buds that weigh 1-15 grams (0.04-0.5 ounces)! Not only will a smaller plant produce the same or more in weight, it will do it in a shorter period of time. A smaller plant, 20 inches (51 cm) or less, can utilize the limited lumens of a CFL better than a large plant because the light is shining over a smaller area.

Not to be able to stop thinking is a dreadful affliction, but we don't realize this because almost everybody is suffering from it, so it is considered normal.
-Eckhart Tolle

DAY 18

*Be kind, for everyone
you meet is fighting
a harder battle.
-Plato*

A mature plant will double and even quadruple in size when its light cycle is changed from 24 hours of light to 12 hours light/12 hours darkness. 95-100% of the vertical growth will occur in the first 2-3 weeks of the 12/12 light cycle. When a plant is forced to flower before it reaches maturity (like this Mango) it more than quadruples its size. Varieties differ greatly in size and growth after inducing flowering. Indicas grow about 25% taller, hybrids 50-100% taller, and sativas double or triple in height. Most of the growth up to this point has affected the Mango's girth more than its height. This bushy growth is a genetic attribute of this Indica strain.

Penalties against possession of a drug should not be more damaging to an individual than the use of the drug itself.

-President Jimmy Carter, message to Congress, Aug. 2, 1977

The red circle (1) indicates secondary growth. The Mango's stems are green and healthy. Each set of new fan leaves is larger than the previous set. Adjustments on the lights are needed daily (up, down, right, left) to keep them as close to the plants as possible, without burning the foliage. The Mango is in the larger pot on the left (3). The two Blue Dots that were started as rooted clones at the same time as the Mango are also doing fabulously.

If you give up the need for security, you will be secure.
-Robert Anthony

DAY
20

Marijuana is the third largest cash crop in America despite law enforcement spending an estimated $30 billion annually to pursue efforts to eradicate the plant.

NORML

Who is the wisest man? He who neither knows or wishes for anything else than what happens.
-Goethe

The Mango was watered with 3.5 quarts of water—a little less than a gallon (3.3 liters). The water's pH was 6.8. The watering was done in 2 phases. 1.75 quarts (1.65 liters) were given to the plant and then 30 minutes later another 1.75 quarts (1.65 liters). This was done so that the water would not over flow from the catch tray below the pot. As usual, the excess water was left in the catch tray. The soil and perlite mixture absorbed the water in about one hour. These stipules are often confused by new growers as pistils or female hairs. Both male and female plants have stipules.

In 2003, 1.3 percent of the USA population were daily marijuana users (i.e., they used marijuana on 300 or more days in the past 12 months).

www.oas.samhsa.gov/2k4/dailyMJ/dailyMJ.htm

The lights in picture (1) were raised for the taking of the photograph. Normally the lights shroud the plants. The Mango is only 6 inches (15.2 cm) tall (2) with an impressive diameter of 16 inches (40.6 cm) (3). It has 6 nodes on the main stalk with a new node sprouting. You can see a leaf tip is burnt from the light being too close (4). The benefits of having the light so close outweighs the damage of this minor burn.

Nobody can hurt me without my permission.
-Mahatma Gandhi

DAY
22

On an annual basis, 1 acre of hemp will produce as much paper as 2 to 4 acres of trees. Global demand for paper will double within 25 years. There is no way to meet future demand without causing massive deforestation and environmental damage. Hemp is the world's most promising source of tree-free paper.

www.hempcar.org/untold-story/hemp_2.html

Ideally, the container is rotated 90° daily to give the plant equal light on all sides. The Mango continues to look great. The leaves are turning towards the light (right). These plants were not rotated because they were being filmed using time lapse photography. You should rotate the plant 90° (a quarter turn) every other day, so the plants get even light.

Marijuana is more popular than politicians. Example: in 2004 Montana voters approved 62% to 38% an intiative to allow medical marijuana use. That year George Bush got 59% percent of the presidential vote. In 2007, Bush's approval rating was a mere 29%, whiile marijuana maintained its popularity.

The process of a plant evaporating water through openings in their leaves is called transpiration. Similar to the respiration process in humans, plants transpire more with increased temperatures, light intensity, water supply, and size. However, if it gets too hot transpiration shuts down. Only 1% of all water a plant absorbs is used in photosynthesis; the rest is lost through transpiration.

Most of us are frightened of dying because we don't know what it means to live.
-Krishnamurti

The right of the people to be secure in their persons, houses, papers, and effects, against unreasonable searches and seizures, shall not be violated, and no Warrants shall issue, but upon probable cause, supported by Oath or affirmation, and particularly describing the place to be searched, and the persons or things to be seized.

The Fourth Amendment to the Bill of Rights of the United States Constitution

We must learn to live together as brothers or perish together as fools.
-Martin Luther King Jr.

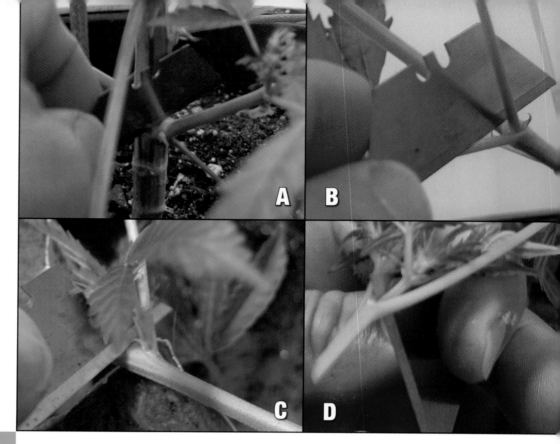

Cloning cannabis is easy. Clones are taken from a plant during its vegetative stage. Some gardeners have mother plants. This Mango did not have any branches big enough to take as clones during its short vegetative stage. The two primary reasons for cloning are: 1. Clones are exact duplicates of the plants which they came from. A female plant insures that the clones will be female. 2. Using clones shortens growing time (skipping the seedling stage). The following are the steps to making clones.

A. Using a clean razor blade, cut one of the lower branches from your plant. Choose a branch that does not get good light exposure and thus will produce little or no buds. Choose a branch that has at least 2 sets of nodes. B. Remove the first set of nodes above your original cut. C and D are also examples of removing the first set of nodes.
NOTE: *Cloning is not necessary, nor may your plants be big enough to clone.*

If an officer asks to search you or an area belonging to you or over which you are authorized to control, you should respond: "I do not consent to a search of my [person, baggage, purse, luggage, vehicle, house, blood, etc.] I do not consent to this contact and do not want to answer any questions. If I am not under arrest, I would like to go now (or be left alone)."

www.norml.org/index.cfm?Group_ID=3405

E-(1). The exposed node after stem's removal; E-(2). A diagonal cut was made ½ inch (1.3 cm) below the exposed node. These exposed areas are most likely where new root growth will occur. F. The clone is dipped in a rooting powder: it is important that the powder covers both exposed areas. G,H. The clone is put into a wet rockwool cube—other grow mediums may be used. It is helpful to put the clones into a container with a clear plastic lid or a cutting tray with plastic domes to keep the humidity level high and increase the success of rooting. (Cutting/germination trays are sold at nurseries.) The clones should be kept between 70-80° F (21-27° C) with a CFL 3-6 inches (7.6-15.2 cm) above them (23-42 watts). Cubes should be kept moist and watered (pH 6.0) by filling the tray with water and allowing the cubes or medium to wick/absorb the moisture (rather than water from the top). Clones usually take 15-20 days to root.

Never let your sense of morals get in the way of doing what's right.
-Isaac Asimov

DAY
25

All the world's a stage, and all the men and women merely players: they have their exits and their entrances; and one man in his time plays many parts.
 -William Shakespeare

You can see where a clone was taken from this Mango plant. Another clone was taken from the other side. This branch was so far below the canopy that it would have produced an insignificant amount of bud. Now that this branch is a clone, it will turn into complete plant of its own!

DAY
26

In the 1970s, a group of teenagers at San Rafael High School in San Rafael, California met every day after school at 4:20 p.m. to smoke marijuana at the Louis Pasteur statue. Evidence supporting an origin of the term from the time 4:20 is the fact that the number is always said "four twenty" This theory is also the most widely accepted.

Rusty brown spots appeared today. This is a possible nutrient deficiency. The spots are only on one leaf; the rest of the plant looks very healthy. This leaf and the other leaves will be monitored very closely.

Out beyond ideas of wrongdoing and rightdoing, there is a field. I will meet you there.
-RUMI

The 1936 propaganda film "Reefer Madness," made to scare American youth away from using cannabis. Today it is seen as a comical farce.

Pot is fun.
-Allen Ginsberg

All the stems look healthy and strong. The nodes have not yet begun to alternate nor has the plant shown any clear signs of its sex. Alternating nodes are a sign of a plant's maturity. The Mango has nine sets of opposing nodes, it is 9 inches (23 cm) tall and has an incredible diameter of 20 inches (51 cm).

Scientists from the Russian city of St. Petersburg have announced they had Managed to develop a new, drug-free variant of cannabis which, if grown on industrial level, would cross with wild growing hemp end eventually force it out of existence.

www.mosnews.com

This AA battery next to the stalk (trunk) of the Mango really brings into perspective just how thick and big this plant has gotten in just 28 days since germination!

*Thoughts are karma.
What are your thoughts?
Watch your thoughts
and you can watch your
karma.
-SeeMoreBuds*

The elusive SeeMoreBuds can sometimes be found on the messageboards at www.rollitup.org.

The plant was given 3.50 quarts (3.3 liters) of water. The water's pH was set to 6.8. The plant was given 1.75 quarts (1.65 liters) and then an additional 1.75 quarts (1.65 liters) 45 minutes later. This is a perfect example of a plant that is thirsty. Notice how soft and droopy the leaves look. From this perspective we should not be able to see the tops of the leaves. We see the tops because the leaves are drooping and the plant is very thirsty. The plant recovered and was perky within two hours of being watered.

Ed Rosenthal is recognized worldwide as a leading authority on marijuana. He has written or edited more than a dozen books about marijuana cultivation and social policy that cumulatively have sold over 2 million copies. At the same time he has been a stalwart defender of all our rights.

Although the Mango has not shown any definitive signs of its sex, it is exhibiting one very positive sign of being a female. This Mango is now only 10 inches (25.4 cm) tall with 10 nodes and an incredible 21 inches (53.3 cm) in diameter. This type of short stout growth is common among female plants.

Meditation is not a method or exercise; rather, it is the condition of presence. It is important not to mistake the menu for the food.
-Krishnamurti

DAY
31

On day 31, exactly 14 days after the Mango's life cycle was switched from the vegeta- tive to the flowering, this Mango revealed it is female. These white hairs known as pistils indicate that the plant is female and capable of producing buds. This also means that the clones that were taken on day 24 are also female. If this plant were male, the plant and the clones would be disposed of immediately. Seeds are not desired by most growers and pollen can ruin a crop. Cannabis plants are either male, female or her- maphrodite. Male and hermaphrodite plants produce pollen which can pollinate the female plant and cause it to produce seeds. If the female plant is not pollinated, the buds will swell and the plant will grow fine sensemilla.

The federal government enacted its first legislation against drug use in 1896. It has been America's longest war, and a total failure for the country, with the exception of those employed in the thankless task of enforcing prohibition.

There was some light leakage from the left side of the closet door. Light leaks are unacceptable and bring unnecessary attention to the garden. Simple errors such as light leaks have ended many gardeners' careers. Some white/black polyethylene (W/B poly) was put up using tape and tacks. W/B poly plastic that is black on one side and white on the other is available at indoor garden shops.

W/B poly is 85% reflective and 100% opaque, making it a great option to use as reflective material and to use to block out light. W/B poly can also serve as plastic lining wherever it is needed. It is very durable and washable.

I discovered this great truth: Unnecessary possessions are just unnecessary burdens.
-Peace Pilgrim

Myth: One joint equals one pack of cigarettes.

http://paranoia.lycaeum.org/ marijuana/facts/mj-health-mythology.html#myth3

When one experiences truth, the madness of finding fault with others disappears.
-Goenka

This is the top of the plant looking down at the main cola. You can see the growth is outstanding and a couple more female pistils have shown themselves. In the next couple of days, white hairs (pistils) will increase 100-fold.

On the "gateway" theory, a federally funded study concluded "there is no conclusive evidence that the drug effects of marijuana are causally linked to the subse-quent abuse of other illicit drugs."

Medicine: Assessing the Science Base," Institute of Medicine, National Academy of Sciences, 1999.

The Mango has had enormous growth since it was put into flowering, 18 days ago. The fan leaves that have opened completely at the top of the plant have seven serrated blades. The next node with emerging fan leaves has nine serrated blades. The foliage is extremely dense and completely obscures view of the stalk. Keeping the lights 3 inches (7.5 cm) from the foliage has kept stretching down to the absolute minimum. The end result will be big BIGGER buds. Light proximity cannot be emphasized enough. Closer is better!

No man is so foolish as to desire war more than peace: sons bury their fathers but in war fathers bury their sons.
-Herodotus

DAY
35

Even if one takes every reefer madness allegation of the prohibitionists at face value, marijuana prohibition has done far more harm to far more people than marijuana ever could.

-William F. Buckley Jr.

Many people excuse their own faults but judge other persons harshly. We should reverse this attitude by excusing others' shortcomings and by harshly examining our own.
-Paramahansa Yogananda

A close look at the newest growth on the main cola reveals an explosion of growth with numerous pistils emerging. All the stems continue to be pure green. Green is good!

After 20 years on the bench, I have concluded that federal drug laws are a disaster. It is time to get the government out of drug enforcement.

Judge Whitman Knapp
Senior U.S. District Judge, 1993

1 **2**

The leaf that was mentioned on day 26 (1) was an isolated incident and these rusty spots were not found on any other leaves. If this discoloration had been treated prematurely and incorrectly it might have caused additional problems.

What you think, you create. What you feel, you attract. What you imagine, you become.
-unknown

DAY
37

Every serious scholar and government commission examining the relationship between marijuana use and crime has reached the same conclusion: marijuana does not cause crime. The vast majority of marijuana users do not commit crimes other than the crime of possessing marijuana.

drugpolicy.org/marijuana/factsmyths

Great minds discuss ideas. Average minds discuss events. Small minds discuss people.
-Eleanor Roosevelt

The main cola has more than 20 pistils. Close attention to the placement of the lights is vital for such dense and fantastic growth.

It costs over $50 billion to incarcerate more than 1.25 million nonviolent prisoners.

http://www.justicepolicy.org/downloads/onemillion nonviolentoffenders.pdf

This is the classic picture of a flowering/budding plant. Clearly, the main cola is most impressive and will produce the largest bud. With proper lighting the buds produced from the smaller branches will also produce significant weight.

Our deepest fears are like dragons guarding our deepest treasure.
-Rainier Maria Rilke

The government assault on Illicit drugs has proved to be a costly failure. We have all been paying the price in misdirected resources, social tension, violent crime, ill health, compromised civil liberties, and international conflict.

The New England Journal of Medicine, Feb. 1994

If the bat desires not union with the sun, the beauty of the sun will not decrease.
-Sa'di

The plant was give 3.50 quarts (3.3 liters) of water. The water's pH was set to 6.8. The plant was given 1.75 quarts (1.65 liters) and then an additional 1.75 quarts (1.65 liters) 45 minutes later. The frequency of watering varies and depends on plant size, temperature and grow medium. The quantity of water given at each watering should be consistent. The temperature in this closet rarely goes over 70° Fahrenheit (21° C). If the temperature were 80° F (27° C), the plant would need twice as many waterings. The top of all the main stems stretched at least 1 inch (2.5 cm) since yesterday. Hopefully the buds will swell and fill in the gaps that are now apparent between the nodes (1). A mosquito (3) was born in the catch tray and sits on one of the Mango's fan leaves. Mosquitoes do not harm plants.

A recent report funded by the Canadian government states that hemp protein is comprised of 66 percent high-quality edistin protein, and that hemp seed contains the highest percentage of this of any plant source.

http://www.nutiva.com/ nutrition/amazing.php

The lower leaves on the plant are beginning to yellow. This is normal for a flowering plant. The plant has no need to sustain these leaves as it completes the final stage of its life cycle.

Weed can get you through times of no money; money cannot get you through times of no weed.
-Fat Freddy

DAY
41

Current police intelligence suggests there are up to 10,000 marijuana grow-ops in the Greater Toronto (Canada) Area.

www.theglobeandmail.com

Is marijuana addictive? Yes, in the sense that most of the really pleasant things in life are worth endlessly repeating.
-Richard Neville

The buds continue to swell daily.

Almost all human and animal studies show that marijuana decreases rather than increases aggression.

drugpolicy.org/marijuana/
factsmyths

You can see that the stem between the nodes is still exposed (1). If this space does not fill up with swollen buds then the grow was not done properly. The 2 smaller plants (2), started as clones and share the same lighting as the Mango. These plants are on the same watering regiment as the Mango. Lower fan leaves continue to turn yellow as the flowering stage progresses.

Nature and wisdom are never at strife.
-Plutarch

DAY
43

According to Forbes.com on April 17, 2007, Harvard University researchers have reported finding that delta-tetrahydrocannabinol (THC), the main psychoactive component of marijuana, reduced the growth of lung cancer in mice.

She has become so tall that the main cola has grown slightly above the lights (1). The lights could be raised but this would distance the bulbs from the other branches. Rather than raise the lights the tip of the stem is gently bent at nearly a 90 degree angle with the help of a simple twisty tie (2,3). Cannabis plants are very easy to train and manipulate but it does require regular adjustments due to the plant's fast growth.

The reason that drugs are illegal is because of the harm they do to individuals particularly. I would think the sensitivity here is because of the harm they do to individuals in a democratic society—that they take away the ability of individuals to act as free, responsible citizens.

-"Drug Czar" John Walters

The first set of fan leaves has turned completely yellow, with the second set not far behind. This can be troubling for new growers, but there is nothing to worry about. This yellowing is very normal and expected from a plant 29 days into flowering. Once a leaf turns completely yellow it will either fall or it can be removed.

Argue for your limitations and sure enough, they're yours.
-Richard Bach

DAY
45

A smoker would have to consume nearly 1,500 pounds of marijuana within about fifteen minutes to induce a lethal response.

www.jackherer.com/comparison.html

The only way to have a friend is to be one.
-Ralph Waldo Emerson

Crystals have begun to form on the leaves.

As reported on May 26, 2006 in the Washington Post and Science Daily, a long term study by UCLA researchers found that marijuana use did not increase the probability of cancer, and suggested that marijuana may have some protective effects against cancer.

The space between the nodes is filling in with swollen buds. The plant is starting to emit a very strong odor which intensifies when it is disturbed. The plant's smell is the strongest one hour before the lights come on.

The greatest challenge I can give you is to dare to be lonely.
-R. Buckminster "Bucky" Fuller, March 20, 1973

DAY
47

Rhode Island legislators resoundingly overrode a gubernatorial veto to make the state's medical marijuana law permanent. Today's 58-11 House vote follows a 29-4 Senate vote to override on Wednesday.

-Providence, Rhode Island, June 21, 2007

If only we'd stop trying to be happy we could have a pretty good time.
-Edith Wharton

Beautiful!

The brain produces its own 'marijuana' to protect neurons, and researchers hope to exploit it to ease anxiety, obesity and addiction.

http://www.digitaljournal.com/article/45475/Interesting_marijuana_research

The Mango has nearly doubled the size of the Blue Dots that are growing beside her. The Mango is 24 inches tall and she will not grow any taller. 80% of the fan leaves show signs of yellowing.

Wisdom is not the product of schooling, but of the lifelong attempt to acquire it.
-Albert Einstein

DAY
49

The active ingredient in marijuana may stall decline from Alzheimer's disease, research suggests.

news.bbc.co.uk/2/hi/health/4286435.stm

You can't have love without justice.
-Abby Hoffman

The plant was given 3.50 quarts (3.3 liters) of water adjusted to 6.8. The plant was given 1.75 quarts (1.65 liters) and then an additional 1.75 quarts (1.65 liters) 45 minutes later.

For the first 162 years of America's existence, marijuana was totally legal and hemp was a common crop.

www.rushessays.com/links.html

The fan leaves on the lower third of the plant, the bottom 6 to 10 inches (15-25 cm), have completely turned yellow, with most becoming necrotic.

My religion is very simple.
My religion is kindness.
-Dalai Lama

DAY
51

Examining marijuana's effects on cognition on 1,318 participants over a 15-year period, researchers reported no significant differences in cognitive decline between heavy users, light users, and nonusers of cannabis. "These results...seem to provide strong evidence of the absence of a long-term residual effect of cannabis use on cognition."

-Johns Hopkins study published in May 1999

1 2

Truth, like surgery,
may hurt, but it cures.
-Han Suyin

The CFL's are meticulously placed around the perimeter of the plant. Having a plant surrounded by lights (1) will provide the grower with several great buds (2). When only top lighting is used, only one or two fabulous colas will form. The bulbs give off light in 360°, making these lights ideal for growing multiple plants in close arrangements.

The human brain naturally produces and processes compounds (anandamides) closely related to those found in Cannabis sativa, better known as marijuana.

-The Brain's Own Marijuana, Roger A. Nicoll & Bradley E. Alger

The main cola is standing straight and has filled out completely. No stem is visible anywhere on the main cola.

When do you learn most? Have you ever watched yourself learning?
-Jiddu Krishnamurti

DAY
53

When young people recognize misinformation about marijuana, they are no longer listening when the facts are presented about more dangerous drugs, and the abuse of these drugs must be our main concern.

-Western Journal of Medicine
Marijuana: A Realistic Approach

Several large colas have formed (1, 2). Large colas could not form without adequate lighting. The four key elements to a successful grow, water, pH, temperature between 70-80° F (21-27 C), close light proximity to foliage, and attention to the plant's needs.

The first evidence for medicinal use of cannabis is an herbal published during the reign of the Chinese emperor Chen Nung 5000 years ago. Cannabis was recommended for malaria, constipation, rheumatic pains, 'absentmindedness,' and female disorders.

-Lester Grinspoon and James Bakalar in *Marijuana: The Forbidden Medicine*

You can see to the right of the Mango, the Blue Dots have grown very nice buds. The lights were also placed 3 inches from the foliage on these plants. The strain's genetics plays a large role in determining the size and growth of a plant's buds.

The art of being wise is knowing what to overlook.
-William James

DAY
55

Sorry, Louis—Gotta Get Back To My Marijuana! George Washington and Ben Franklin were in France raising money for the Revolution. Washington told the King of France that he had to return to Virginia. He said, "I wouldn't miss the hemp harvest at Mount Vernon for all the tea in China." Hemp was used to make clothes and paper. It was the number one cash crop of the colonies until the invention of the cotton gin.

www.civil-liberties.com

A man will renounce any pleasure you like but he will not give up his suffering.
-Gurdjieff

Some of the upper fan leaves are beginning to lose their solid green appearance. The main cola's heavy weight has caused it to lean.

Personal correspondence and records reveal that Presidents Jefferson, Madison, Monroe, and others smoked hashish, as did Benjamin Franklin and Mary Todd Lincoln. President John F. Kennedy smoked marijuana to relieve his back pain.

Sources: National Archives, published reports. http://www.erowid.rg/plants/cannabis/cannabis_flyer1.shtml

The buds have nearly reached full size. The biggest change in the buds between now and harvest time will be the transformation of pistil color, from white to reddish brown.

Insanity is extending one's identity beyond the body.
-unknown

DAY
57

Drug War—The term itself was coined in 1971 by Richard Nixon to describe a new set of initiatives designed to enhance drug prohibition.

wikipedia.org/wiki/War _on_Drugs

Reality is what you have left when you stop thinking.
-unknown

More and more pistils turn from white to reddish brown everyday. This color change is the normal maturation process of buds and signifies the end of the flowering stage.

Marinol (dronabinol) is the only US FDA approved synthetic cannabinoid. It is often marketed as a legal pharmaceutical alternative to natural cannabis.

Many of the yellowing and necrotic leaves have been pulled from the plant. The removal of dead leaves increases air flow and increases light penetration. Fungus and molds grow in cool temperatures—55-70° F (13-21° C). This is especially true when there is high humidity, stagnant air and low light. A very promising plant can quickly be destroyed by mold or fungus.

Breath is the bridge which connects life to consciousness, which unites your body to your thoughts.
-Thich Nhat Hanh

DAY
59

Rat pups genetically engineered to not produce the endogenous cannabinoid anandamide cannot suckle, and die if not given marijuana supplementation.

-reported by Dr. Esther Fride

This may be the last day of watering. The plant was given 4 quarts (3.8 liters) of water adjusted to a pH of 6.8. The plant was given 2 quarts (1.9 liters) and then an additional 2 quarts (1.9 liters) 45 minutes later.

After rigorous study,
Dr. Lester Grinspoon
reported that marijuana
causes hysteria—in people
opposed to its use.

These three colas are impressive in size, aesthetic, and number of crystals.

*We will not learn how to
live together in peace
by killing each other's
children.*
-Jimmy Carter

DAY
61

Marijuana is a green, brown, or gray mixture of dried, shredded leaves, stems, seeds, and flowers of the hemp plant (Cannabis sativa).

FALSE INFORMATION PRESENTED TO THE PUBLIC ON THE OFFICE OF NATIONAL DRUG CONTROL POLICY WEBSITE. SHOULDN'T THEY KNOW WHAT THEY ARE TALKING ABOUT?

The first casualty when war comes is truth.
-Hiram Johnson

Nearly all the remaining fan leaves are yellow.

I'm for total legalization, but it won't happen until 2010, after the Bush presidency.

-Ed Rosenthal

Sooner or later the desire and craving to eat the buds will come to you. When they look like this, how can you not want to eat them! The smell by now is unmistakable to any grower. Although guests in the vicinity of your garden may think the odor is a skunk.

The smell is very potent. Many varieties of plants will give off a strong odor about one hour before the lights come on during the final 4-6 weeks of flowering. It is important to recognize the strength of this odor and take appropriate actions to hide it when necessary.

The more laws and order are made prominent, the more thieves and robbers there will be.
-Lao Tzu

Percentage of population using marijuana at least once a month—as reported by their governments:

1. New Zealand   22.23%
2. Australia   17.93%
3. United States   12.30%
4. United Kingdom   9.00%
5. Switzerland   8.50%
6. Ireland   7.91%
7. Spain   7.58%
8. Canada   7.41%
9. Netherlands   5.24%
10. Belguim   5.01%

www.nationmaster.com

When nothing is for sure we remain alert, perennially on our toes. It is more exciting not to know which bush the rabbit is hiding behind than to behave as though we knew everything.
-Carlos Castenada

She is so sticky! If you touch her and then touch something else, the item will stick to your hand. You will not be able to easily rinse away the smell or the stickiness after touching the plant in this stage of its life

Reported percentage of population using marijuana in the last month (top 10 states):

1.	Alaska	15.83%
2.	Vermont	14.90%
3.	Rhode Island	14.85%
4.	New Hampshire	14.60%
5.	Massachusetts	14.19%
5a.	Washington D.C.	13.81%
6.	Colorado	13.32%
7.	New Mexico	13.25%
8.	Oregon	13.18%
9.	Montana	12.80%
10.	Michigan	12.61%

www.statemaster.com

She has grown beyond her parent's expectations. A true beauty, with one major cola and five minor colas. Many growers that use expensive, high energy consumption HID lighting do not get these results. HID lighting creates a lot of heat. Rather than manage the heat, many growers raise the lights furthering the distance between the HID light and the plants. Raising the lights defeats the purpose of using HID lighting. When HID lighting is used at the correct distance from a plant with exhaust and cooling systems, the results are amazing.

If you want to make God laugh, tell him your plans.
-unknown

DAY
65

We believe … that the continued prohibition of cannabis jeopardizes the health and well-being of Canadians much more than does the substance itself or the regulated marketing of the substance.

-Canadian Senate Special Committee on Illegal Drugs 2002

Gardening requires lots of water – most of it in the form of perspiration.
-Lou Erickson

About 40% of the hairs have now changed from white to reddish brown. The few remaining fan leaves are becoming brittle and easily falling off.

All persons who spent jail or prison time for cannabis equals 14 million years in aggregate.

-Jack Herer, *The Emperor Wears No Clothes*

It is important that the lights do not touch any of the buds. It is not ideal but definitely okay if a fluorescent light touches and burns the tip of a leaf. It is NOT acceptable for any light to touch the buds. The light will burn the bud and damage valuable herb! If the light burns the bud before it is done growing, it will most likely stunt the buds growth.

Tug on anything at all and you'll find it connected to everything else in the universe.
-John Muir

DAY
67

Since mandatory minimum sentencing began for drug offenders, the Federal Bureau of Prisons' budget has increased from $220 million in 1986 to $4.8 billion in 2008.

www.mpp.org

60% of the hairs have changed color. The main cola (pictured) is taking the longest to mature. This is not always the case. Often the top of the plant will mature quicker than the lower parts of the plant. Some gardeners will harvest the plant in sections over the duration of 1-14 days. Side lighting definitely promotes more even ripening of a plant.

The Government Account-ability Office (GAO) has found that the $1.4 billion anti-drug advertising campaign managed by the drug czar's office, ONDCP, doesn't work.

stopthedrugwar.org, 2007

69 days ago the seed cracked. Today she is harvested. She is cut at her lowest point where her stalk greets the soil. All the larger leaves are removed. She is turned upside down and hung from a clothes hanger. She will stay in this dark closet for 5-10 days. When she is almost completely dry she will be taken down and manicured even further. Then she will be put into a large zip lock bag or glass jar. The container will be sealed for 24-48 hours and then reopened for 6-12 hours. This opening and closing process lets out unwanted moisture. This is repeated until the bud reaches the desired conditions. If she gets too dry, a piece of fresh parsley can be added to the container before sealing it. If there is too much moisture in the container and it is not allowed to breathe, she can grow mold on her and destroy the smoke.

The sun, with all those plants revolving around it and dependent upon it, can still ripen a bunch of grapes as if it had nothing else in the universe to do.
-Galileo

DAY
69

ONDCP (drug czar's office) has 111 full-time employees. The director, John Walters, earns $273,000 a year. He heads the $70 billion per year drug prohibition industry.

Clearly express love every day. And practice expressing love in every moment.
-SeeMoreBuds

Examining the buds.

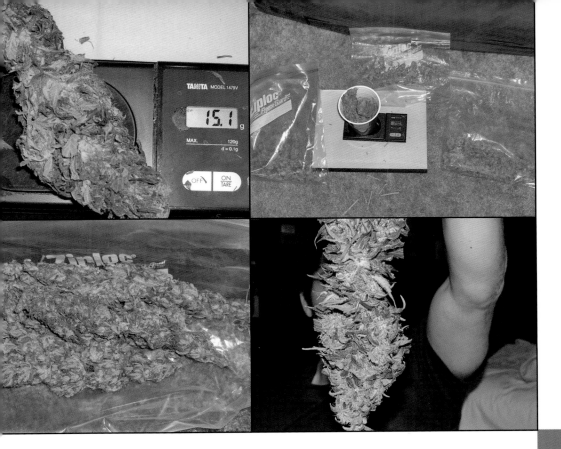

In 1937, when the government passed their first anti-marijuana law, there were 55,000 users. Now there are 55 million users, an increase of 10,000%. At this rate, around 2030 there will be more marijuana users in the U.S. than there are people. You say how can this be? It's the pets.

-Ed Rosenthal

After a 6-day drying period, the final measurements are in. This single Mango plant yielded just over 3 ounces of dried herb. This included a monster main cola weighing 15.1 grams (.53 ounces). The 2 Blue Dots yielded a total of 5 ounces making the entire harvest just over a half pound of chronic!

I love pot the most.
-Tom Forcade

Closing—

It is of great importance that the grow is done safely, and with enjoyment. Do not let the growing process bring negativity into your life, regardless of failure or success. All growers experience unexpected broken branches, bug infestations and other obstacles. Remember you are growing for enjoyment and you are in control of your own happiness!

SeeMoreBuds (SMB) was born in Oakland, California and dwelled in the San Francisco Bay area his entire life. Until 1992 when SMB left to go to college, he was a real Momma's boy and reptile aficionado.

During SMB's 7 year stint as an undergrad at the University of California Santa Barbara, he studied black studies, communication and film. During his 4th year at the University, 1994, he outgrew the Momma's boy stage and started to dabble in marijuana cultivation and female admiration. This interest grew, as did SMB's reputation in the California underground gardening scene.

In 1997, while in a 5-day silent meditation, he had a moment of enlightenment and realized love for all of humanity. From 1997 to 1999 SMB walked the earth in an ecstatic bliss. Service for the elderly became his calling in 1999, to which he devoted all of his attention until 2004.

In 2004, SMB released a feature length documentary, produced and directed more than 15 television shows, and did sports casting on ESPN (under another name).

In 2005, SMB released "SeeMoreBuds, 15 lbs. in 80 days." 2006 was a great year—his DVD got great recognition in the underground grow scene and SMB was also acknowledged by the Guru of Ganja, Ed Rosenthal. SMB has made 2 follow up DVDs "SeeMoreBuds, Growing Marijuana Volume 2" (2006) and "SeeMoreBuds, The Perfect Garden" (2008).

Although SMB has a very busy schedule that has taken him to more than 5 continents, 40 countries and all 50 states, he finds time to exercise and meditate daily. Besides love for all of humanity, physical and mental strength is the most important element in SeeMoreBuds' life.

SeeMoreBuds can often be seen playing frisbee on Santa Barbara, California beaches and hanging out on the message boards at www.rollitup.org.

Other best sellers from Quick Trading: Available at bookstores everywhere, and online @ www.quicktrading.com

GROW YOUR OWN

Big Book of Buds..Ed Rosenthal

Big Book of Buds 2..Ed Rosenthal

Big Book of Buds 3..Ed Rosenthal

Closet Cultivator ....Ed Rosenthal

Easy Marijuana Gardening ....Ed Rosenthal

Marijuana Growers Handbook ....Ed Rosenthal

Marijuana Flower Forcing .... Tom Flowers

Marijuana Hydro Gardens............................ Tom Flowers

Marijuana Success Indoors...........................Ed Rosenthal

Marijuana Success Indoors V.2 ....Ed Rosenthal

Grow Like A Pro ....Dana Larsen

Organic Marijuana Soma Style .... Soma

Cultivating Exceptional Cannabis ....DJ Short

POPULAR CULTURE

Ask Ed Marijuana Gold..................................Ed Rosenthal

Joint Rolling Handbook 2 ....Bobcat

Marijuana Herbal Cookbook .... Tom Flowers

Stir Crazy..Bobcat

MUSHROOMS

Psilocybin Mushroom Handbook.................... Nicolas, Ogamé

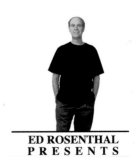

ED ROSENTHAL
P R E S E N T S

www.quicktrading.com

METRIC CONVERSION

Mass

1 gram = 0.035 ounces (1/28 ounce)
1 ounce = 28.35 grams
1 pound = 16 ounces
1 kilogram = 2.2 pounds
1 pound = 0.45 kilograms

Length

1 foot = 30.5 centimeters (1/3 meter)
1 meter = 3.28 feet
1 meter = 100 centimeters
1 inch = 2.54 centimeters

Area

1 square meter = 10.76 square feet
1 square foot = .09 square meters

1 ounce per square foot = 305 g per square meter
100 grams per square meter = 0.33 oz. per square foot

Temperature

$15°C = 59°F$
$20°C = 68°F$
$25°C = 72°F$
$28°C = 82°F$
$30°c = 86°F$
$32°C = 89.5°F$
$35°C = 95° F$

To figure:

Celsius = (F - 32) x 5/9
Fahrenheit = C x 9/5 + 32

Notes